SANTA'S LITTLE HELPERS

A True Tale of Giving and Joy

By

Sheila O'Brien

Illustrated by Kyle Bateman

Paperback ISBN: 979-8-3305-0656-9
Hardcover ISBN: 979-8-3305-0645-3

Editing and layout by Self-Publishing Services, LLC (selfpublishingservices.com)
Illustrations by Kyle Bateman

Printed in Missoula, MT

Dedication

Dedicated to the Community Ladies and the kids of Philipsburg, Montana.

And to my friends Debbie and Sarah,
who encouraged me to put this poem into a children's book.

In a small Montana town, where the Christmas lights are all aglow,
and the mountains, tree tops and streets are covered with sparkling snow

There's a special day that the children like to remember.
It's not the day you are thinking of,
because this special day takes place in mid-December.

The children look forward to playing Santa at this event,
choosing gifts for each family member for only 25 cents.

The local brewery hosts a fundraiser,
which brings in donations and lots of cheer,
and the local grocery store provides brown paper bags each year.

The Community Ladies and volunteers hunt for deals throughout the year.
They look for gifts and trinkets galore,
and shop at rummage sales, thrift shops, and online discount stores.

On a cold fall day, the Community Ladies and volunteers who are able
listen to Christmas songs and cut out old Christmas cards,
while sitting around an oak kitchen table.

The Christmas cards are cut in a pattern of zig-zag
and then glued on a small, medium, or large brown paper bag.

The Community Ladies and volunteers meet at the school the day before,
and spread the school and volunteer fire department tables
across the gymnasium floor.

The children are overwhelmed when they see the tables covered with gifts,
but then smiles come across their faces
and they take out their Christmas gift lists:

A camouflage hat for dad or a shiny new tool,
A pink pair of gloves for mom or a new necklace covered in jewels,

A stuffed brown teddy bear for sister
or a set of crayons and a new coloring book,
A coffee mug for Grandpa or some fishing bobbers and hooks,

A toy car for brother or a mini football,
A scented candle for Grandma or a Christmas angel to hang on her wall,

A catnip filled mouse, for the cat at home,
or for a dog, a blue squeaky toy shaped like a bone.

Then each gift is placed in a decorated bag,
and the to and from is written by the child as the holiday gift tag.

The Christmas card bags are stapled closed, then carefully packed,
and the children look like Santa carrying their gift-filled sacks.

When they arrive home, they place their gifts
around the Christmas tree on the floor,
and then say "THANK YOU" to the Philipsburg Kids Christmas Store!

Merry Christmas!

Thank-You Notes From Student Shoppers

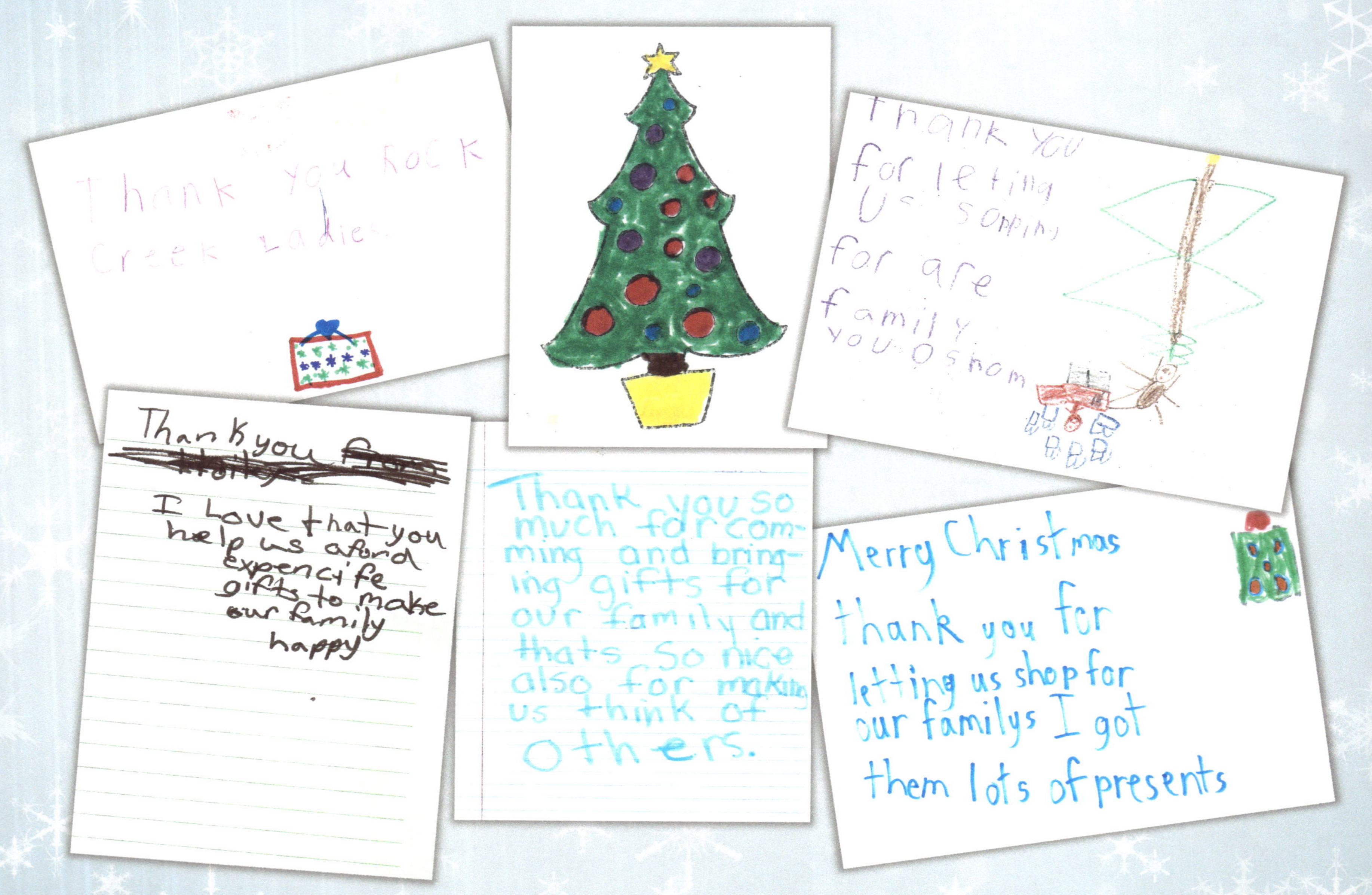

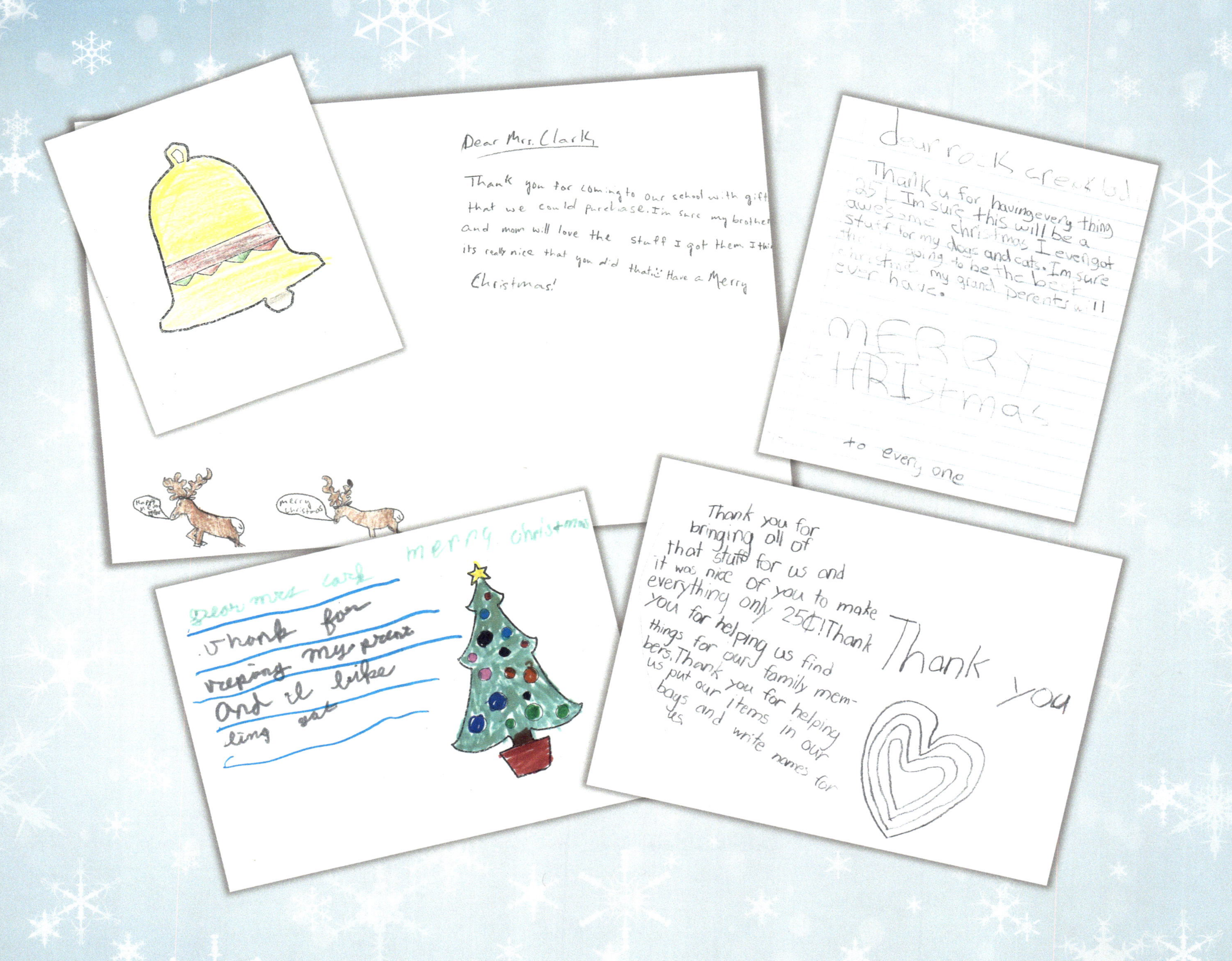

Dear Mrs. Clark
Thank you for coming to our school with gift
that we could purchase. I'm sure my brother
and mom will love the stuff I got them I thi
its really nice that you did that.:: Have a Merry
Christmas!

dear rock creek bs!
Thank u for having every thing
.25¢ I'm sure this will be a
awesome christmas. I even got
stuff for my dogs and cats. I'm sure
this is going to be the best
christmas my grand perents will
ever have.
MERRY
CHRISTMAS
to every one

Happy new year
merry christmas

merry christmas
Dear mrs clark
Thank for
reping my present
And il like
ling sat

Thank you for
bringing all of
that stuff for us and
it was nice of you to make
everything only 25¢! Thank
you for helping us find
things for our family mem-
bers. Thank you for helping
us put our items in our
bags and write names for
us
Thank you

A History of the Philipsburg Christmas Store

In 1980, Philipsburg resident Barbara Clark was inspired by a magazine article about someone gathering gently used clothing and shoes and then selling them inexpensively at a sale for children in need. Barbara wanted to recreate the idea for a Christmas sale at the Philipsburg Elementary School. She liked the idea that the items would be priced affordably, but not free, because she wanted the children to have the joy of ownership, of picking something out and spending their own money on it.

The first year or two, Barbara did it all. She would gather things from her house and local yard sales. She enlisted her husband to look for useful things he no longer used in his shop or work. (Gifts for fathers have always been hard!) The first year, nothing was very official—just a little sale at the elementary school during lunch. Not many kids showed up, so wrapping was easy enough.

The sale grew over the next couple of years with help from the teachers and a neighbor or two. The community took to calling it the Kid's Christmas Sale Store. For several years, Barbara and her helpers wrapped all the presents the children bought. It started to get very busy! Barbara's daughter, Sheila Walden, remembers helping with her best friend during their junior high lunch hour. They just put their heads down and wrapped!

The sale took a break for a few years in the late 80s to early 90s, but it wasn't forgotten. One day Carol Winninghoff, a remarkable local lady, told Barbara it was time to restart the sale, so they did.

Again, Barbara recruited her friends and neighbors. This time everyone remembered how wonderful the sale had been, and it was larger than ever! Carol was a tireless collector of treasures (still is), and Barbara and her husband shopping each holiday season out of their own pockets for enough things for the sale. They would buy items wherever they found the best deals. They even bought batteries to put in the flashlights! Over the years, Barbara and the community ladies learned helpful things, like setting up in the gymnasium, not selling breakable or overly large items, and decorating brown paper bags to use instead of wrapping paper—it saved so much time!

The sale continues today with the help of Barbara, Carol, and many volunteers from Rock Creek and beyond. Some like to shop for items to sell, and some like to help with the organized chaos of sale day, but all love to see the excitement in the children's eyes. One young shopper even left a nickel tip one year! Some of the gifts are still provided out of the volunteers' pockets and from donations, and an annual fundraiser at the local brewery helps cover costs, too.

Today, children whose parents remember shopping for that special Christmas gift at our sale years ago line up to buy their own presents, and the magic goes on!

ABOUT THE AUTHOR

Sheila O'Brien has been involved with the Philipsburg Kids' Christmas Store for over 10 years.

Her passion for the store began when she witnessed firsthand the joy and excitement it brought to children in the Philipsburg community. Since then, she has been an integral part of the event, dedicating countless hours to ensuring its success.

Sheila's love for the store extends beyond volunteering her time. She takes great pride in helping to shop for the unique and affordable items that fill the store's shelves, ensuring that every child has the opportunity to find the perfect gift for their loved ones.

One of Sheila's favorite aspects of the store is crafting the decorative bags that the children use to carry their presents home.

Sheila's dedication to the Philipsburg Kids' Christmas Store stems from her deep-rooted belief in the power of community and the importance of giving back. She is honored to play a role in this cherished tradition, and she looks forward to continuing her involvement for many years to come.